HAL•LEONARD
INSTRUMENTAL
PLAY-ALONG

 AUDIO ACCESS
INCLUDED

Songs from
Frozen, Tangled
and Enchanted

CONTENTS

To access audio visit:
www.halleonard.com/mylibrary

Enter Code
2378-0316-9385-1972

Audio Arrangements by Peter Deneff

ISBN 978-1-4803-8724-9

Disney characters and artwork © Disney Enterprises, Inc.

WALT DISNEY MUSIC COMPANY
WONDERLAND MUSIC COMPANY, INC.

DISTRIBUTED BY

HAL•LEONARD®
CORPORATION
7777 W. BLUEMOUND RD. P.O. BOX 13819 MILWAUKEE, WI 53213

In Australia Contact:
Hal Leonard Australia Pty. Ltd.
4 Lentara Court
Cheltenham, Victoria, 3192 Australia
Email: ausadmin@halleonard.com.au

Visit Hal Leonard Online at
www.halleonard.com

DO YOU WANT TO BUILD A SNOWMAN?

from Disney's Animated Feature FROZEN

TENOR SAX

Music and Lyrics by KRISTEN ANDERSON-LOPEZ
and ROBERT LOPEZ

3

FOR THE FIRST TIME IN FOREVER

from Disney's Animated Feature FROZEN

TENOR SAX

Music and Lyrics by KRISTEN ANDERSON-LOPEZ
and ROBERT LOPEZ

HAPPY WORKING SONG

from Walt Disneys Pictures' ENCHANTED

TENOR SAX

Music by ALAN MENKEN
Lyrics by STEPHEN SCHWARTZ

I SEE THE LIGHT

from Walt Disney Pictures' TANGLED

TENOR SAX

Music by ALAN MENKEN
Lyrics by GLENN SLATER

I'VE GOT A DREAM

from Walt Disney Pictures' TANGLED

TENOR SAX

Music by ALAN MENKEN
Lyrics by GLENN SLATER

11

IN SUMMER
from Disney's Animated Feature FROZEN

TENOR SAX

Music and Lyrics by KRISTEN ANDERSON-LOPEZ
and ROBERT LOPEZ

LET IT GO

from Disney's Animated Feature FROZEN

TENOR SAX

Music and Lyrics by KRISTEN ANDERSON-LOPEZ
and ROBERT LOPEZ

LOVE IS AN OPEN DOOR

from Disney's Animated Feature FROZEN

TENOR SAX

Music and Lyrics by KRISTEN ANDERSON-LOPEZ
and ROBERT LOPEZ

MOTHER KNOWS BEST

from Walt Disney Pictures' TANGLED

TENOR SAX

Music by ALAN MENKEN
Lyrics by GLENN SLATER

SO CLOSE
from Walt Disney Pictures' ENCHANTED

TENOR SAX

Music by ALAN MENKEN
Lyrics by STEPHEN SCHWARTZ

Moderately, with feeling

THAT'S HOW YOU KNOW
from Walt Disney Pictures' ENCHANTED

TENOR SAX

Music by ALAN MENKEN
Lyrics by STEPHEN SCHWARTZ

TRUE LOVE'S KISS
from Walt Disney Pictures' ENCHANTED

TENOR SAX

Music by ALAN MENKEN
Lyrics by STEPHEN SCHWARTZ

WHEN WILL MY LIFE BEGIN
from Walt Disney Pictures' TANGLED

TENOR SAX

Music by ALAN MENKEN
Lyrics by GLENN SLATER